USBORNE FIRST READING
Level Three

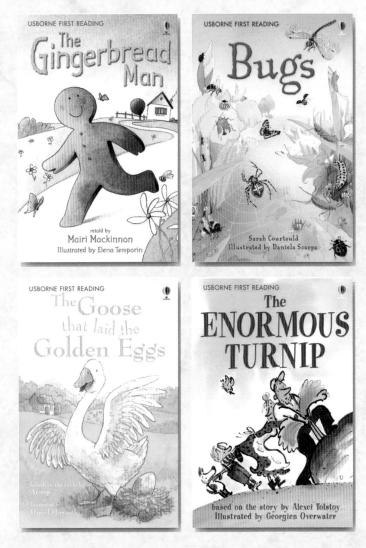

USBORNE FIRST READING

The Gingerbread Man

retold by
Mairi Mackinnon
Illustrated by Elena Temporin

USBORNE FIRST READING

Bugs

Sarah Courtauld
Illustrated by Daniela Scarpa

USBORNE FIRST READING

The Goose that laid the Golden Eggs

based on the fable by
Aesop
Illustrated by
Daniel Howarth

USBORNE FIRST READING

The ENORMOUS TURNIP

based on the story by Alexei Tolstoy
Illustrated by Georgien Overwater

Bugs

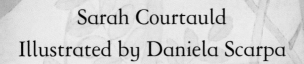

Sarah Courtauld
Illustrated by Daniela Scarpa

Reading Consultant: Alison Kelly
Roehampton University

Wherever you look...

...you can find lots and lots of creeping, crawling animals called bugs.

3

There are millions of
different kinds of bugs.

Shiny
beetles,

hairy
spiders,

4

buzzing
dragonflies,

furry
caterpillars...

and many,
many more.

5

Some bugs live in water.

Some flutter
through the air.

7

And some bugs live
all alone in holes in
the ground.

Others live together
in enormous nests.

9

There are
bugs as long
as your arm

and bugs that
are almost too
small to see.

11

A blade of grass looks like
a huge tree to a tiny bug...

...but these tiny bugs can leap far above the grass

up, up, up

into the air.

Many bugs have hard
shells. All bugs have six
legs or more.

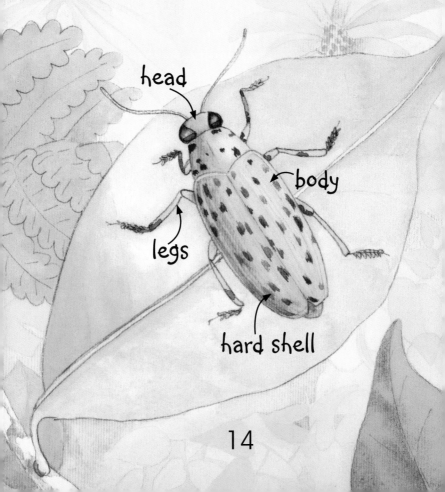

head

body

legs

hard shell

Spiders have
eight legs.

Centipedes
have dozens of
wriggly legs.

15

Many bugs have
big eyes.

But they don't see what
we see. This is how the
world looks to a bee.

Bugs find their way
around with long feelers.

feelers

18

They smell things with
their feelers too,

and find
tasty food.

19

Leaf cutter ants smell
leaves with their feelers.

They pick them up and
carry them home to eat.

21

Bees make their own food.
They suck sugar from
flowers...

and carry it
back to their hive.

Then they turn the sugar
into honey to eat

and save it
up for winter.

23

Some bugs eat other bugs.
A spider spins a long,
silky web.

A fly buzzes into the
web and gets stuck.

The spider gobbles
up the juicy fly.

Other animals eat bugs
too. But bugs use tricks
to escape.

This bug looks
just like a leaf.

A bird is looking for bugs
to eat. It can't see any.

The bug stays still
and the bird flies away.

Birds like eating
caterpillars...

...but not this one.
It has big red spikes.

The sharp spikes don't
look good to eat.

The bird flies off and
the caterpillar is safe.

29

Bugs grow up fast. Then
they rush out to find
a partner.

Grasshoppers
find partners by
rubbing their legs.

30

This makes a noise that goes chirrup chirrup

so other grasshoppers find them.

31

Fireflies find a partner by shining. They glow like little stars.

The males fly to the
females...

and they get into pairs.

Wolf spiders find a partner by dancing. But they have to be careful. If they make a wrong move...

their partner
might eat them up.

35

Once the bugs are in
pairs, the female bug
lays lots of eggs.

Butterflies don't take
care of their eggs.

They fly off
right away.

When baby bugs are
born, they are very, very
hungry.

They eat and eat...

and grow bigger...

and
bigger.

These bugs have grown
too big for their shells.

They burst
out of them.

There are shiny,
new shells underneath.

Some bugs change shape
as they grow. Dragonflies
are born underwater.

They grow larger
and crawl onto land.

They shed
their skins

and soar
into the air.

43

There are wriggling, leaping and flying bugs all around you.

Look outside.
How many can you see?

45

Bug words

Here are some of the words
in the book you might
not know.

hive - a place where
bees live

web - a silk net
made by a spider

feelers - long stalks
on a bug's head

Index

eggs, 36-37

eyes, 16-17

feeding, 19-25, 35, 38-39

feelers, 18-20

flying, 7, 32-33, 43

nests, 9

shells, 14, 40-41

water bugs, 6, 42

Bug websites

You can find out more about bugs by going to the Usborne Quicklinks Website at www.usborne-quicklinks.com and typing in the key words "first reading bugs". Then click on the link for the website you want to visit.

The recommended websites are regularly reviewed and updated but, please note, Usborne Publishing is not responsible for the content of any website other than its own. We recommend that young children are supervised while on the internet.

Edited by Susanna Davidson

Designed by Katrina Fearn

Series editor: Lesley Sims

Consultant: Matt Shardlow,
Director of Buglife,
The Invertebrate Conservation Trust

First published in 2007 by Usborne Publishing Ltd., Usborne House, 83-85 Saffron Hill, London EC1N 8RT, England. www.usborne.com
Copyright © 2007 Usborne Publishing Ltd.